RISKY JOBS

POLICE OFFICER

JENNA TOLLI

PowerKiDS press

Published in 2025 by The Rosen Publishing Group, Inc.
2544 Clinton Street, Buffalo, NY 14224

First Edition

Editor: Jenna Tolli
Book Design: Rachel Rising

Photo Credits: Cover, LightField Studios/Shutterstock.com; Cover, pp. 1, 3–24 Apostrophe/Shutterstock.com; Cover, pp. 1, 3–24 ReVelStockArt/Shutterstock.com; Cover, pp. 1, 4, 6, 12, 14, 20, 22-24 cobalt88/Shutterstock.com; p. 5 FeyginFoto/Shutterstock.com; p. 6 a katz/Shutterstock.com; p. 8 Nadezda Murmakova/Shutterstock.com; p. 9 jan kranendonk/Shutterstock.com; p. 10 Phase4Studios/Shutterstock.com; p. 11 Fractal Pictures/Shutterstock.com; p. 12 CLP Media/Shutterstock.com; p. 13 YAKOBCHUK VIACHESLAV/Shutterstock.com; p. 14 Aquarius Studio/Shutterstock.com; p. 15 New Africa/Shutterstock.com; p. 17 bibiphoto/Shutterstock.com; p. 18 Billy Watkins/Shutterstock.com; p. 19 Roxane 134/Shutterstock.com; p. 21 Kilmer Media/Shutterstock.com.

Library of Congress Cataloging-in-Publication Data

Names: Tolli, Jenna, author.
Title: Police Officer / Jenna Tolli.
Description: Buffalo, New York : PowerKids Press, [2025] | Series: Risky jobs | Includes index.
Identifiers: LCCN 2024006244 (print) | LCCN 2024006245 (ebook) | ISBN 9781499446135 (library binding) | ISBN 9781499446128 (paperback) | ISBN 9781499446142 (ebook)
Subjects: LCSH: Police-Vocational guidance–Juvenile literature.
Classification: LCC HV7922 .T66 2025 (print) | HV7922 (ebook) | DDC 363.2023/73–dc23/eng/20240216
LC record available at https://lccn.loc.gov/2024006244
LC ebook record available at https://lccn.loc.gov/2024006245

Manufactured in the United States of America

CONTENTS

PROTECTING THE COMMUNITY

Police officers are men and women hired to **protect** communities throughout the country. Their duties are to patrol, or move through, neighborhoods to watch out for trouble. Police officers are meant to **enforce** laws, answer calls for help, and respond to **emergencies**. When a crime happens, they are called to investigate, or look for answers. They may need to arrest people who are breaking the law.

Being a police officer can be a dangerous job. There are risks when they are working. They may see some scary things. They can be hurt or killed while doing their job.

DANGER!

The Federal Bureau of Investigation (FBI) reported 118 U.S. law enforcement officers died in the line of duty in 2022.

Police officers are also known as law enforcement officers.

HOW TO BECOME A POLICE OFFICER

Police officers get special training to do their jobs. First, they need to take an exam, or test, to see if they have what it takes to become a police officer. If they pass, they go to a special school called the police academy.

At the police academy, people learn how to handle things that might happen when they are on duty. This includes how to drive police cars, how to make an arrest, how to use a gun, and more. There are police academies all over the country. On average, someone in the police academy completes over 800 hours of training.

DANGER!

Police academies don't just teach officers about using **equipment** in the field. They're also supposed to teach ideas like ethics, or what is right and wrong. This is very important.

When police officers graduate from the police academy, they take an oath. An oath is a promise that says they're supposed to be honest and treat people with respect.

SPECIAL EQUIPMENT

Police officers carry different kinds of equipment while they are on duty. Most police officers in the United States carry a gun, extra bullets, and handcuffs. They also have radios to call for help and give updates to other officers.

Bulletproof vests can help protect officers. They are made of **materials** like Kevlar. These are strong but light enough to wear on your chest. They can help stop bullets or knives. Some officers who work in some dangerous situations might wear helmets or face shields. Body armor can also help them.

Some police officers will use bicycles or horses to get around. These can help them in crowds.

ON PATROL

Police officers usually patrol many areas. This means they walk or drive around neighborhoods to watch for things. They look for activities they think are **suspicious** and people who might be in danger. They're also supposed to get to know people and places in the areas they patrol. This can build trust and may help keep communities safe.

Sometimes police officers chase people on roads or highways. This can mean they drive very fast. Chasing people and traveling at high speeds can lead to car **accidents**. Police officers can also get hurt by other cars when they are talking to someone they have pulled over.

Other cars and people on the road are also in danger during a police chase.

DRUG ENFORCEMENT

There are different units, or groups, in police departments. Some units are responsible for drug enforcement. They're supposed to **investigate** and enforce laws related to illegal drugs. They're supposed to find and arrest people who sell drugs.

Police officers look into who deals drugs and who works with them. They're meant to keep track of illegal activity and catch people breaking the law. Officers might go undercover to build a case to arrest people. When a police officer goes undercover, it means they pretend to be someone else.

DANGER!

Police dogs can help find drugs. Groups of police officers who work with police dogs are called K-9 units. They also look for **weapons**, missing people, and more.

Sometimes drug enforcement units carry out raids to find drugs. A raid is a surprise or sudden attack by law enforcement officers.

BLENDING IN

Sometimes police officers and **detectives** wear everyday clothes when they are on duty. This helps them blend into crowds. They are also called plainclothes officers.

Police officers might go undercover to investigate possible crimes. Going undercover means they don't act like a police officer or dress in a police uniform. They may try to get close to people who break the law. This may help undercover police catch criminals, or someone guilty of a crime. Police who go undercover need special training and skills to do this part of their job.

DANGER!

If a police officer sees a crime when they are not working, they might jump in to help in an emergency. They're supposed to quickly identify themselves to people.

Plainclothes officers might also do surveillance, which means they closely watch someone.

SWAT: SPECIAL WEAPONS AND TACTICS

Sometimes police officers face very dangerous situations with weapons, **threats** to public safety, or hostages. Hostages are people illegally held by force by someone else.

Police may call in a SWAT team for these kinds of situations. "SWAT" stands for "special weapons and **tactics**." These teams often handle the most dangerous cases. They handle situations that may need a lot of force. If police officers think that someone has a gun and other people are in danger, they might call in the SWAT team. The SWAT team can help find and arrest the person who is making threats.

Police officers who are in SWAT units may carry powerful guns called sniper rifles.

PATROLLING THE WATER

Police officers who work near lakes, rivers, or coasts also use boats to patrol the water for many reasons. They may be called the water police, port police, or river police.

These units handle emergencies that happen in the water. This includes search and rescue work, or SAR. SAR units are trained to rescue, or save, people from the water. Sometimes police divers go into the water to search for missing people. There are dangers to working in the water, especially when it's freezing. It can also be hard to see underwater when they are working at night.

Police dive teams have training to practice their skills. They need to learn how to help people get out of the water safely while keeping themselves out of danger.

PROTECT AND SERVE

Every day, police departments are ready to respond to crimes. They need to be available 24 hours a day for any emergency. Their jobs can be dangerous and come with risks.

To be a police officer, you need training. Some people decide to become police officers because they want to serve their community. Many police officers feel committed to their positions and the work they do.

One police saying is "to protect and to serve." Police are supposed to do the right thing and protect people. This can be a risky job!

DANGER!

Did you know that some police departments have ride-along programs? Adults and some teenagers can ride with a police officer during the day to learn about their work.

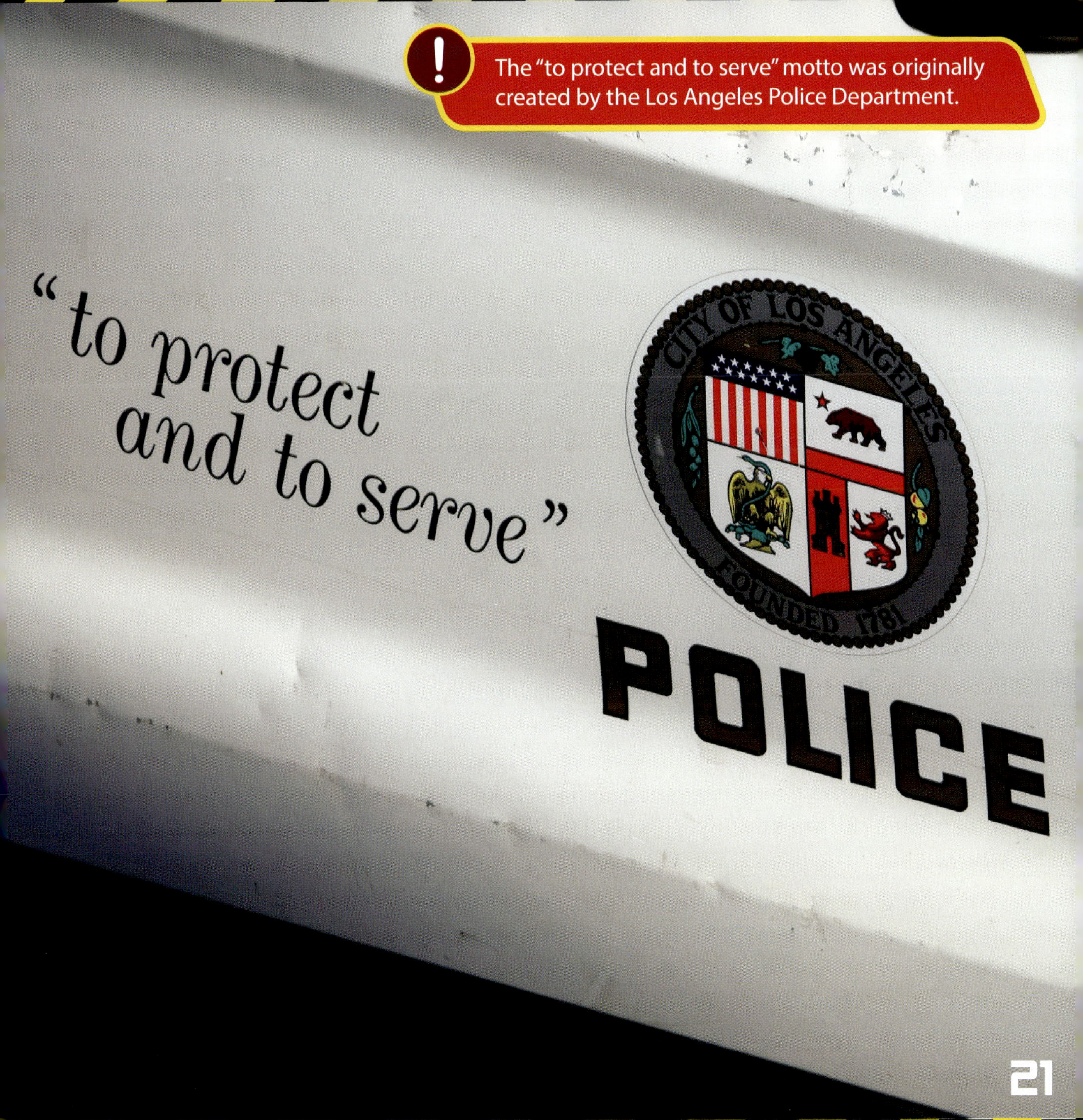

The "to protect and to serve" motto was originally created by the Los Angeles Police Department.

GLOSSARY

accident: An unexpected and sometimes bad event.

detective: People who find out the facts and figure out who did crimes.

emergency: An unexpected situation that calls for immediate action.

enforce: To put or keep in force.

equipment: All the supplies needed to do something.

investigate: To study by closely examining.

material: What something is made of.

protect: To keep safe.

suspicious: Causing a feeling that something is wrong.

tactic: A plan to do something that requires special skills.

threat: A person or thing that may cause others to be hurt or killed.

weapon: An object used to hurt or kill.

FOR MORE INFORMATION

BOOKS

Honders, Christine. *Why Should I Listen to Police Officers?* New York, NY: Rosen Publishing, 2019.

Hudak, Heather C. *Police Force Careers.* New York: Crabtree Publishing Company, 2021.

WEBSITES

Junior Police Academy
juniorpoliceacademy.org
Learn how police departments across the country work with young people.

National Child Safety Council
nationalchildsafetycouncil.org
Learn how the National Child Safety Council works with police officers and law enforcement.

New York City Police Department
www.nyc.gov/site/nypd/index.page
Read about the largest police department in the United States, the New York City Police Department (NYPD).

INDEX